NORTH AMERICAN ANIMALS

Golden Eagles

by Christina Leighton

BELLWETHER MEDIA • MINNEAPOLIS, MN

BLASTOFF! READERS
3

Note to Librarians, Teachers, and Parents:

Blastoff! Readers are carefully developed by literacy experts and combine standards-based content with developmentally appropriate text.

Level 1 provides the most support through repetition of high-frequency words, light text, predictable sentence patterns, and strong visual support.

Level 2 offers early readers a bit more challenge through varied simple sentences, increased text load, and less repetition of high-frequency words.

Level 3 advances early-fluent readers toward fluency through increased text and concept load, less reliance on visuals, longer sentences, and more literary language.

Level 4 builds reading stamina by providing more text per page, increased use of punctuation, greater variation in sentence patterns, and increasingly challenging vocabulary.

Level 5 encourages children to move from "learning to read" to "reading to learn" by providing even more text, varied writing styles, and less familiar topics.

Whichever book is right for your reader, Blastoff! Readers are the perfect books to build confidence and encourage a love of reading that will last a lifetime!

This edition first published in 2017 by Bellwether Media, Inc.

No part of this publication may be reproduced in whole or in part without written permission of the publisher. For information regarding permission, write to Bellwether Media, Inc., Attention: Permissions Department, 5357 Penn Avenue South, Minneapolis, MN 55419.

Library of Congress Cataloging-in-Publication Data

Names: Leighton, Christina, author.
Title: Golden Eagles / by Christina Leighton.
Other titles: Blastoff! Readers. 3, North American Animals.
Description: Minneapolis, MN : Bellwether Media, Inc., 2017. | Series:
   Blastoff! Readers. North American Animals | Audience: Ages 5-8. |
   Audience: K to grade 3. | Includes bibliographical references and index.
Identifiers: LCCN 2016032043 (print) | LCCN 2016044216 (ebook) | ISBN
   9781626175679 (hardcover : alk. paper) | ISBN 9781681032887 (ebook)
Subjects: LCSH: Golden eagle–Juvenile literature.
Classification: LCC QL696.F32 L45 2017 (print) | LCC QL696.F32 (ebook) | DDC
   598.9/423–dc23
LC record available at https://lccn.loc.gov/2016032043

Editor: Betsy Rathburn   Designer: Brittany McIntosh

Table of Contents

Golden eagles are large **raptors**. These birds fly over most of North America.

N
W E
S

Extinct

Extinct in
the Wild

Critically
Endangered

Endangered

Vulnerable

Near
Threatened

Least
Concern

golden eagle range = ▢

conservation status: least concern

They are seen from Mexico to northern Canada. They are Mexico's national bird.

Size of a Golden Eagle

average human

golden eagle

6
5
4
3
2
1
(feet)

Golden eagles can weigh
15 pounds (7 kilograms).
They are up to 3 feet
(1 meter) tall.

Their wings may stretch more than 7 feet (2 meters) across! Females are bigger than males.

These eagles have hooked beaks with black tips. They are named for the golden feathers on their heads and necks.

feathered ankles

hooked beak

golden head

Dark brown feathers cover the rest of their bodies. The birds even have feathers on their ankles!

Golden eagles have excellent eyesight. These **carnivores** can see **prey** from far away.

gray squirrels

grouse

jackrabbits

prairie dogs

red foxes

white-tailed deer

They search for food high in the sky or on a **perch** in the distance. They often hunt **mammals** or find **carrion**.

These birds are **swift** hunters. They can fly more than 150 miles (241 kilometers) per hour!

When golden eagles spot prey, they dive. Then they grab their meal with their **talons**.

talons →

Nesting Pairs

Golden eagles usually live alone or in pairs. In winter, some **migrate** south for the season.

In spring and summer, pairs
perform **courtship displays**.
They dance and chase each
other in the sky.

Together, a pair builds a huge nest on a cliff or a tree branch. The nest takes about a month to finish.

A pair often returns to the same nest year after year. Some golden eagles stay together for life.

Female golden eagles lay up to four eggs. Both parents watch over the eggs and keep them warm. The babies hatch a little over a month later. The babies chirp and grow.

Baby Facts

Name for babies:	eaglets
Number of eggs laid:	1 to 4 eggs
Time spent inside egg:	42 days
Time spent with parents:	3 to 5 months

The parents take turns feeding the **eaglets**. The babies hop around the nest and stretch.

They become **fledglings** after about ten weeks. Now they are ready for their first flight!

Glossary

carnivores—animals that only eat meat

carrion—the rotting meat of a dead animal

courtship displays—behaviors that animals perform when choosing mates

eaglets—baby eagles

fledglings—young birds that have feathers for flight

mammals—warm-blooded animals that have backbones and feed their young milk

migrate—to travel from one place to another, often with the seasons

perch—a high place from which a golden eagle can watch for prey

prey—animals that are hunted by other animals for food

raptors—large birds that hunt other animals; raptors have excellent eyesight and powerful talons.

swift—able to move quickly and suddenly

talons—the strong, sharp claws of golden eagles and other raptors

To Learn More

AT THE LIBRARY
Bowman, Chris. *Bald Eagles*. Minneapolis, Minn.:
Bellwether Media, 2015.

Hill, Melissa. *Golden Eagles*. North Mankato, Minn.:
Capstone Press, 2015.

Macken, JoAnn Early. *Golden Eagles*. Pleasantville,
N.Y.: Weekly Reader Pub., 2010.

ON THE WEB
Learning more about golden eagles
is as easy as 1, 2, 3.

1. Go to www.factsurfer.com.

2. Enter "golden eagles" into the search box.

3. Click the "Surf" button and you will see a
   list of related web sites.

With factsurfer.com, finding more
information is just a click away.

Index

The images in this book are reproduced through the courtesy of: davemhuntphotography, front cover; Martin Mecnarowski, p. 4; My Good Images, p. 4 (background); FLPA/ Alamy Stock Photo, p. 7; yykkaa, p. 8; Raimon Santacatalina, p. 9 (top left); Gary Blakeley, p. 9 (top center); TTstudio, p. 9 (top right); Vladimir Kogan Michael, p. 9 (bottom); Ondrej Prosicky, p. 10; Michael Rowlandson, p. 11 (top left); Eurospiders, p. 11 (top right); Erni, p. 11 (center left); Gerald A. DeBoer, p. 11 (center right); Eric Isselee, p. 11 (bottom left); JAMES PIERCE, p. 11 (bottom right); Bildagentur Zoonar GmbH, p. 12; Richard Constantinoff, p. 13; J Peltomaeki/ Age Fotostock, p. 14; Markus Varesvuo/ Nature Picture Library, p. 15; cla78, p. 15 (background); Uno Berggren/ ardea.com/ Age Fotostock, p. 16; Philip Mugridge/ Alamy Stock Photo, p. 17; Lane V. Erickson, p. 17 (background); CSP_dbvirago/ Age Fotostock, p. 18; Fulashay, p. 19; REUTERS/ Alamy Stock Photo, p. 20; spaugh, p. 21.